THE DEATH OF CINEMA

The Rosetta Stone. Grey and pink granodiorite stela, issued March 27, 00196 BC. British Museum.

THE DEATH OF CINEMA

History, Cultural Memory and the Digital Dark Age

PAOLO CHERCHI USAI

 Publishing

English edition first published 2001
by theBritish Film Institute
21 Stephen Street, London W1T 1LN

The British Film Institute promotes greater understanding of,
and access to, film and moving image culture in the UK.

Designed and set in Fournier MT TC by Ketchup, London
Printed in England by The Cromwell Press, Trowbridge, Wiltshire

Printed on acid-free Fineblade Smooth 130gsm. This paper meets the requirements of ISO 9706:1994,
Information and documentation – Paper for documents – Requirements for permanence, and
American National Standard ANSI/NISO Z 39.48:1982 – Permanence of paper for publications and
documents in libraries and archives. The pulp is sourced from sustainable forest.

Cover Image: *Body Snatchers* (Abel Ferrara, 01994). Frame enlargement from a 35mm acetate
print. George Eastman House.

British Library Cataloguing-in-Publication Data
A catalogue record for this book is available from the British Library
ISBN 0 85170 837 4 (paperback)
ISBN 0 85170 838 2 (hardback)

CONTENTS

PREFACE

In a symposium held in the late summer of 1980 at the Venice Film Festival I spoke about the tragedy of colour degradation in the movies and made a call for action to prevent the further destruction of such a crucial component of our motion picture heritage. Had I known how much worse the situation was going to turn out in the years to come, I would have probably expressed myself in more dramatic terms. But how could I imagine that the colours of *Taxi Driver*, made only five years earlier, were already fading and needed urgent restoration? How could we know that contemporary cinema was as much in danger as the films made in the first half of the 20th century? At the time, the term 'vinegar syndrome' (now commonly used to designate the degradation of acetate motion picture film) had not even been invented by film archivists. All we knew was that prints were starting to shrink, become curled, and would be unprojectable by the time their penetrating, unpleasant acidic smell had reached almost unbearable levels. Convinced as I was that the main weapon at our disposal was the duplication of nitrate film onto a more stable medium, I encouraged archives to do so at a faster rate by supporting their efforts and endorsing their fundraising endeavours.

Much progress has been made since then. More film is being preserved than ever. More governments and granting agencies are involved in this challenge. Filmmakers such as Robert Altman and Clint Eastwood have joined The Film Foundation, which I established in 1990 with nine other eminent artists like Francis Ford Coppola, Steven Spielberg, and Stanley Kubrick, to raise funds and awareness of the urgent need to preserve our motion picture history. Film preservation has become a relevant item in the cultural agenda of our times. There are now schools teaching how to preserve films, such as the L. Jeffrey Selznick School of Film Preservation, held at George Eastman House, where Paolo Cherchi Usai operates. There are more efficient techniques to prolong the longevity of the film after restoration, from molecular sieves to slow down the vinegar syndrome process, to the creation of climatised vaults where films are being kept at better and more stable levels of temperature and humidity. Archives and laboratories know how to restore films better than they ever did before. Digital technology is certainly not a substitute for motion picture stock when it comes to the preservation of the original cinematic experience and the conservation of the film artifact, but it surely can help in facilitating the work of those who attempt at bringing back the moving image to its original glory.

Like all good things, however, the worthwhile cause of film preservation can be (and has been) abused in the name of commercial interests. The very term 'preservation' and 'restoration' are being indiscriminately appropriated by marketing experts who know nothing about preservation itself but are aware of the economic potential of its public appeal. Many of the films made available today through electronic media are misleadingly hailed as 'restored', while nothing really has been done to enhance their chances to be brought to posterity. No less damaging than the 'vinegar syndrome', the mystique of the restored masterpiece is condemning to obscurity thousands of lesser-known films whose rank in the collective memory has not yet been recognised by textbooks. (When I located a 35mm print of a favourite film of my childhood, *Fair Wind to Java*, it became painfully clear that no decent printing element existed for this Republic Pictures' 'B' picture, shot in Trucolor. It is currently being restored at UCLA with support from The Film Foundation.)

Finally, the critical role played by conservation in the mission to preserve the film heritage is still largely unrecognised by the public opinion. Somehow, audiences are being led to believe that digital will take care of it all with no need for special storage conditions. Indeed, spending money on the restoration of *Lawrence of Arabia* makes the donor as happy as the spectator watching the preserved film. While spending one hundred times as much for the construction of a refrigerated vault is of vital importance to keep the negative and print in good shape, there's no glamour about it. For years I have been working with Paolo at the conservation of my own films at the George Eastman House, and know how frustrating his task can be when it comes to bringing this unrewarding and yet essential feature of film preservation to public attention. But this is nothing compared to the massive tragedy of all the moving images that are already lost to us forever. There will be no vaults for them, and no fundraising effort will ever bring them back to us.

This book is an elegy to the thousands copies of films being destroyed every day, all over the world, due to the lack of a global conservation strategy and the blatant indifference of some governments and the very same people who once paid money to make those films available to all. Paolo has drawn with clinical precision (and a welcome touch of irony) the picture of a worldwide crisis that commands our unconditional concern. His portrait of a culture ignoring the loss of its own image is a devastating moral tale: there is something very wrong with the way we are taught to dismiss the art of seeing as something ephemeral and negligible.

Martin Scorsese
Rome, September 2000

INTRODUCTION

I had never seen a book torn to shreds in public until two years ago, when Francesco Casetti, a distinguished film theorist who happens to be a dear friend, and had volunteered to present an earlier version of this volume at the Cineteca Italiana in Milan on October 11, 01999 stunned the audience (and the publisher) by ripping off its pages, adding that 'there's no better way of reading this work'. He perfectly understood what this book is about. All the same, I can't think of a more appropriate way to summarise how some of the thoughts contained in it have been received over the years in their various incarnations – first as a *jeu d'esprit* for a journal of film theory, then as a more serious piece of business for the moving image preservation field, and finally as an attempt to explain why the argument at their core uses the term 'digital' as little more than a pretext for bringing the pleasures of controversy to a broader set of issues.

Back in 01977, at the time of my first experience in a film archive, I realised how little had been done to save the motion picture heritage, and was eager to enter the fray of repairing that neglect. Ten years later, I was at the peak of enthusiasm at the prospect of a collective effort to restore the cinema of the past to its original glory through the endeavours of film preservation. Another decade has passed, and the much touted benefits of the Digital Revolution have quickly shifted towards a subtle yet pervasive ideology. There's something inherently reactionary in how worldwide consensus has been gathered around this new myth of scientific progress. What's worse, denouncing its excesses will make *you* feel like the latest anti-technologist on the block. The subtitle of this book derives from Stewart Brand's *The Clock of the Long Now* (01999), the most effective attempt at questioning this self-perpetuating wave of cultural fundamentalism; however, much of the argument addressed in the pages that follow has different roots, and comes from a variety of directions, not necessarily linked to the digital persuasion. Why are we producing so many images that move and speak? Why do we try to preserve them? What do we think we are doing by presenting them as pristine reproductions of our visual heritage? Why is our culture so keen in accepting the questionable benefits of digital technology as the vehicle for a new sense of history?

An indirect proof of how unsettling these questions can be is given by the multiple titles this book has had in its previous printings. It began as *A Model Image*, and it seemed obscure to most readers, but digital was not quite yet the talk of the town; it turned into *Decay Cinema* and then *The Last Spectator*, thus raising the suspicion that the whole point of the book was some sort of Remembrance of Cinematic Things Past; it finally became *The Death of Cinema*, a concept we had been hearing of for a long time but dreaded to mention. The acid-free paper should make it slightly more difficult to tear the book apart in the future, but as far as I'm concerned the option still exists for those who have read it all the way through.

So why is it that a text written over fifteen years ago has not only refused to die, but has actually grown upon itself like a plant, into a wealth of amendments, rewrites and rethinkings? The fact is that I was unable to abandon it, and fortunately there were those who felt I should persist. Michèle Lagny made it all happen in 01986, and is too modest to claim credit for it; Michele Canosa brought it to its first Italian translation in 01989, not without some personal risk. Roland Cosandey understood the project well enough to bring to my attention an 01897 notice from *La Nature*, knowing I could not resist the temptation of placing it at the head of this work, and I thank him for that. Simonetta Bortolozzi had no cultural agenda at stake, a fortunate coincidence that made her remarks and suggestions the most useful I've had in relation to the essay in its present form. The diagrams in Sections IX and XXIX are adapted from drawings by Stewart Brand and Brian Eno for the 01998 website of the Long Now Foundation (www.longnow.org).

The latest stages of the project have been blessed by two remarkable guardian angels. Renata Gorgani, director of the publishing company Il Castoro, of Milan, has believed in this project since she first read the manuscript, and it is thanks to her that it has now emerged exactly as it was intended. For this English (and revised) edition, Martin Sopocy has generously given his time, patience and editorial skills in helping me express what I wanted to say more effectively than I could ever have hoped. They have both understood that if I had to throw away everything I have written so far, and save only one thing from the bonfire, it would be this book. Now it belongs to them.

Rochester, New York, September 02000

THE DEATH OF CINEMA

The great creator is the great eraser.

Stewart Brand

Edison Kinetophone, 01895–01900. George Eastman House.

It is not generally appreciated how much research and labour is sometimes expended, in the industrial sector, to produce results that are often quite ephemeral. We find a new instance of this (following that of rapid-fire weaponry, which we cited about two years ago) in the individual photographs of the kinetoscope and the cinematographe. In the kinetoscope, each tiny photograph that is paraded past the onlooker's view was exposed and subsequently put to use for only 1/7000 of a second. Now before being retired from active service these bands can scarcely be run 4000 or 5000 times. As a result, the real and active life-span of each tiny image is somewhat less than a second. In the case of the cinematograph, the duration of exposure is longer: it lasts as long as 2/45 of a second, 15 images being exposed every second, each of them appearing for 2/3 of a 15th of a second. In contrast, by virtue of the jerky movement to which the strip of film is subjected, it can survive its passage through the apparatus scarcely more than 300 times before being retired from active service. As a result of all this, its effective life is in its totality one-and-one-third seconds. One knows, a priori, that a piece of fireworks is ephemeral. Its has, even so, an effective life incomparably longer than a projectile fired by a mechanical weapon or the cinematographe's projected photograph, because it lasts several seconds. However paradoxical it may seem, this conclusion is quite rigorous; it can be confirmed by a simple bit of arithmetic, and is yet another instance of how dangerous it is to trust appearances.

Anon., 'La vie utile des vues cinématographiques', *La Nature* (Paris), 01897, 2ème semestre, pp. 302–3. Translated by Paolo Cherchi Usai and Martin Sopocy.

I
Cinema is the art of moving image destruction

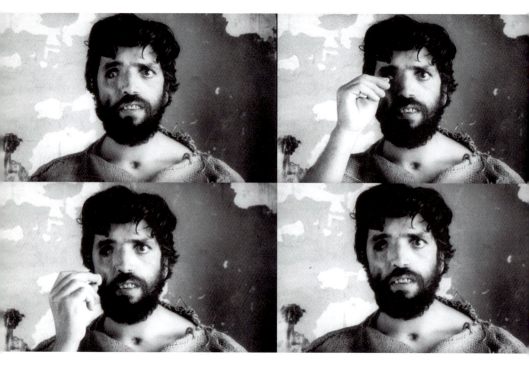

Lo zio di Brooklyn (Daniele Ciprì and Franco Maresco, Italy 01995). Frame enlargements from a 35mm acetate print.

Without the images of drama, adventure, comedy, natural and artificial events imprinted on motion picture film there would be no cinema; there would be nothing to make history out of; filmology would have nowhere to go. In its place would be either still images (photography) or fleeting ones (electronics). The point is confirmed by video: a civilization that is prey to the nightmare of its visual memory has no further need of cinema. For cinema is the art of destroying moving images.

II
Is cinema the object of history?

The Bombing of Shanghai South Station by the Japanese, filmed by Hai-Sheng 'Newsreel' Wong for Hearst Metrotone News on August 27, 01937. *News of the Day*, Vol. 9, No. 200, released September 15, 01937. Courtesy of Blaine Bartell, Hearst Metrotone Newsreel Collection at the UCLA Film and Television Archive.

No. As we conceive it, film history does not allow us to assess, predict, or modify the process of moving image destruction. Cinema has never had a historiography capable of fully expressing itself beyond the stage of the quantitative, of classifying, of the strictly explicatory, of the simple chronicle of the presence or absence of constants and variables, further disfigured by value judgments and self-projected intentions. One may give it the attributes of history only by employing the term in its narrowest sense.

III

Is cinema a potential object of history?

Lotte Reiniger, *Die Abenteuer des Prinzen Achmed* (01922). George Eastman House.

Yes. The Model Image is its ideal type.

IV
The moving image disgraced

Persona (Ingmar Bergman, 01960). Frame enlargements from a 35mm print. Courtesy of Harvard Film Archive.

In addition to the factors which can prevent its coming into being (malfunction of the apparatus, inadequate processing of the negative or its accidental exposure to light, human interference of various kinds) there is the host of physical and chemical agents affecting the image carrier: scratches or tears on the print caused by the projecting machine or its operator, curling of the film base as the result of a too intense exposure to the light source, colour alterations arising out of the film stock itself, environmental variables such as temperature and humidity. As soon as it is deposited on a matrix, the digital image is subject to a similar destiny; its causes may be different, but the effects are the same. Chronicles also mention catastrophes and extraordinary events such as fires, wars, floods, and destructive interventions from the makers themselves or the people who finance their activities.

V
Tentative correlations

Back staircase, British Film Institute, 21 Stephen Street, London. Security video, March 22, 02001.

Our inquiry should begin by establishing a preliminary set of correlations between the destruction of moving images and the physical or chemical factors that determine the structure of the image carriers. As their preservation and decay arise from the conditions under which such images are produced and exhibited, an effort to evaluate the way in which those conditions affect the aesthetic and pragmatic nature of the viewing experience ought to be made. At its outset film history tentatively fits within this framework of analysis, unless it becomes tainted by sociology, by statistics, and by a mindless search for visual and narrative recurrences.

VI

The unfortunate spectator

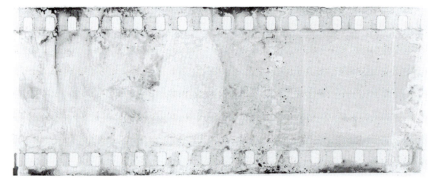

Unidentified decomposed film, ca. 01925. Reel 4. Frame enlargement from a 35mm nitrate print. George Eastman House.

Given the physical and chemical phenomena at the heart of the process of decay [IV], a process that can be contained or decelerated but not altogether avoided, the viewer is an unconscious (sometimes resigned, in any case impotent) witness to the extinction of moving images that nobody cares to preserve, either because they are deemed unworthy [XXXVIII] or unsuitable for the purposes of further commercial exploitation. This is considered as normal as the corruption of an oral tradition, or the vanishing of other ephemeral forms of human expression.

VII

It is the destruction of moving images that makes film history possible

A nitrate film storage room after a fire. Unidentified location, United States, ca. 01920. Academy of Motion Picture Arts and Sciences.

That is to say, the Present is indivisible and overwhelming, while the Past presents us with a limited set of choices on which to exercise such knowledge as we are able to glean from the range of perspectives that remain [XLIV]. If all moving images were available, the massive fact of their presence would impede any effort to establish criteria of relevance – more so, indeed, than if they had all been obliterated, for then, at least, selective comprehension would be replaced by pure conjecture.

VIII
The iconoclasts

An employee of the Douglas Fairbanks Studio chopping up 'useless' film (01922).
Courtesy of the National Center for Film and Video Preservation.

The axiom presented in [VII] is also applicable to film taken as a single entity, usually perceived as a totality even when some of its parts are forever unknown to the viewer's experience of it. Film history proceeds by an effort to explain the loss of cultural ambience that has evaporated from the moving image in the context of a given time and place. The diverse conditions determining this loss create the need to establish periodisations in the history of moving image destruction and in the human effort to destroy images altogether. If all moving images could be experienced as a Model Image (that is, in their intended state, in an intention visible in every part of them even before their actual consumption), no such thing as film history would be needed or possible.

IX
The moving image in history

In August 01999 the estate of Abraham Zapruder received the sum of $16,000,000 for the 8mm film depicting the assassination of John F. Kennedy in Dallas, Texas, November 22, 01963 – the largest amount ever paid for a motion picture artifact. *JFK* (Oliver Stone, 01991) makes use of this footage in a fictional account of the investigation on the event by multiplying Zapruder's 486 frames in a plethora of duplicates, slow-motion enlargements and re-enacted versions. Ironically, this analytical approach results in a fragmented catalogue of ambiguities, making the original document all the more elusive.

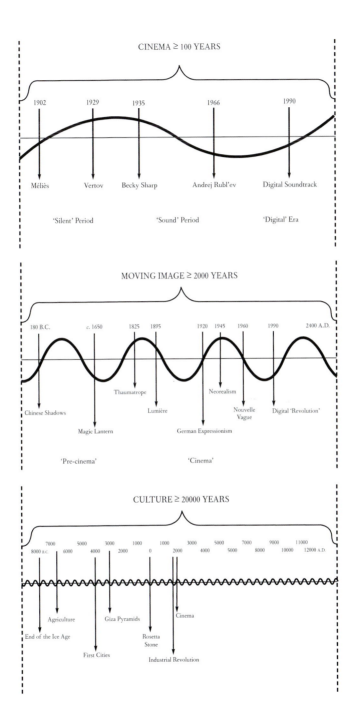

CINEMA ≥ 100 YEARS

| 1902 | 1929 | 1935 | 1966 | 1990 |

Méliès Vertov Becky Sharp Andrej Rubl'ev Digital Soundtrack

'Silent' Period   'Sound' Period   'Digital' Era

MOVING IMAGE ≥ 2000 YEARS

180 B.C.   c. 1650   1825   1895   1920   1945   1960   1990   2400 A.D.

Thaumatrope   Neorealism

Chinese Shadows   Lumière   Nouvelle   Digital 'Revolution'
                                            Vague

Magic Lantern   German Expressionism

'Pre-cinema'   'Cinema'

CULTURE ≥ 20000 YEARS

7000   5000   3000   1000   1000   3000   5000   7000   9000   11000
8000 B.C.   6000   4000   2000   0   2000   4000   5000   8000   10000   12000 A.D.

Agriculture   Giza Pyramids   Cinema

End of the Ice Age   Rosetta
                            Stone

First Cities

Industrial Revolution

X
Primary goal of film history

Maciste (Romano L. Borgnetto, 01915). Frame enlargement from a 35mm nitrate print. Nederlands Filmmuseum.

The subject of film history being the destruction of the moving image, its primary goal is to recapture the experience of its first viewers, an empirical impossibility. If put into practice such reconstruction would lead to the obliteration of film history. Its objectives are thus as abstract as any political utopia: neither would have any interest whatsoever if their goals were realised.

XI
Origins of film theory

Ivan Groznij [Ivan the Terrible, Part I] (Sergei M. Eisenstein, 01944). Frame enlargement from a 35mm acetate print. Courtesy of Kristin Thompson.

Theories of film are constructed upon the disgraced moving image. Unlike histories of film, however, their aims are generally prescriptive; hence their ideological rationale. Film theory, too, would cease to exist in face of a Model Image.

XII
The perfect vision

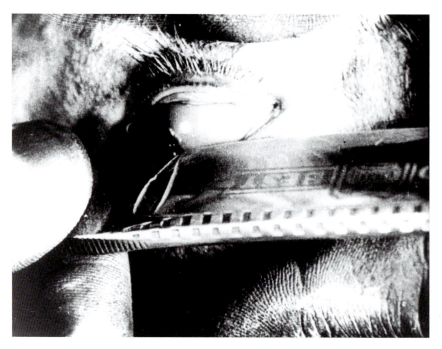

Un Chien andalou (Luis Buñuel and Salvador Dalí, 01928). British Film Institute.

The perfect vision has no duration and is not durable. This axiom is at the heart of the notion of film history.

XIII
The moving image is no evidence

A victim of Bergen-Belsen, filmed on April 16, 01945, following the liberation of the con-
centration camp. (Cameraman: Sgt Mike Lewis, British Army Film and Photographic
Unit.) Imperial War Museum, London. Negative number IWM FLM 3272.

Nature and social life are perceived by cinema as a sequence of events that can be remembered. Moving images produced outside the world of fiction give identity to the viewing experience as fragments of empirical evidence, but they can prove nothing unless there is some explanation of what they are. Be it ever so eloquent, the moving image is like a witness who is unable to describe an event without an intermediary. The ability to transform it into evidence, true or false [XL], is inherently linked to a decision to preserve, alter or suppress the memory of the circumstances under which the image was produced. The loss of the moving image is the outcome of an ideology expressed by the very object that made it possible.

XIV
The urge to create visions

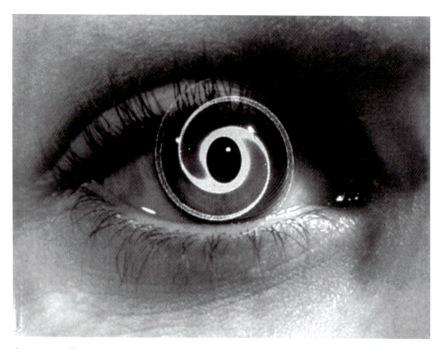

A rotating silhouette drifts across the right eye of Kim Novak in the main credits of *Vertigo* (Alfred Hitchcock, 01958). Reticular entities in motion endowed with shifting colours are perceived when the eyelids are closed; it can therefore be said that humans never cease to see moving images in the course of their lives. These 'mental' images, known as phosphenes, are described in some detail by the German visionary, musician, writer and theologican Hildegard von Bingen (01098–01179) in her mystical writings. Saul Bass's opening sequence has often been interpreted as a symbolic reference to the emotional twists experienced by the characters in the film. Strictly defined, the term 'vertigo' refers to an illusion or a hallucination of movement. When the symptom complex is of spinning or rotation, the cause is almost always the inner ear or its peripheral vestibular system. Although it is true that people affected by vertigo experience a definite sense of environmental spin or self-rotation, the majority are not subject to true spinning vertigo.

Visionary cinema has no other subject matter than the transformation of the image itself, for otherwise it would have nothing to exercise itself upon. Whether the outcome is cheerful or tragic (but also in the lack of a narrative pattern), the event that results is a self-obliterating illusion that is doomed sooner or later to fade into the realm of memory.

XV
How do moving images come to exist?

[*Kindertentoonstelling*] (probably *Concorso di bellezza fra bambini a Torino*, Aquila Films, Turin 01909). Frame enlargement from a 35mm nitrate print. Nederlands Filmmuseum.

Experience teaches us that loss of memory is as inevitable as anxiety for the future. In the hopes of avoiding both, the maker of moving images fabricates memories or visions of what is to come in the cherished belief that they will exist forever in an eternal present of the spectator's will. Exposing the spectator to a single viewing of that moving image is enough to reveal the futility of such ambition.

XVI
Comedy

Maluco e mágico (William Schoucair, Filmarte, Brasil 01927). Frame enlargement from a 35mm print. Cinemateca Brasileira.

When the maker of moving images smiles and shows contempt for being remembered, we call his despair comedy.

XVII
The potential image

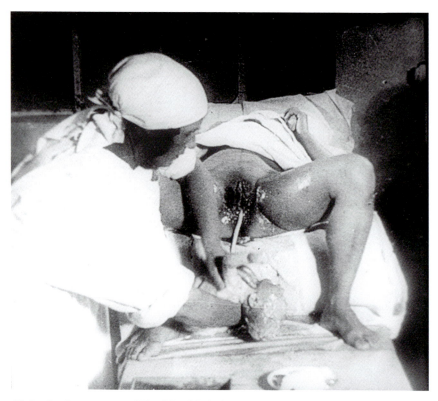

Chelovek s kinoapparatom [The Man With the Movie Camera] (Dziga Vertov, 01929).
Frame enlargement from a 35mm acetate print. George Eastman House.

It may be possible to imagine the existence of a moving image as it goes through the process of being created. This hypothetical condition can be defined as a potential moving image. Once it has been projected, the film resulting from this intention is subject to the physical decay of its images and the memory of perfection lost, thus giving birth to the history of cinema.

XVIII
The Golden Age: the Model Image

35mm SMPTE leader, designed in the 01960s by the Society of Motion Picture and Television Engineers. The countdown footage which precedes the beginning of a film (from 8 to 2 seconds before the image or its soundtrack) was first introduced in the United States on November 01931 ('Academy' countdown leader), and it is used worldwide in a variety of designs.

Such an hypothesis is based upon the existence of moving images which are immune from decay. By definition, such images can have no history.

XIX
The Model Image, commercially defined

Unidentified early cinema façade. British Film Institute.

The economic factors determining the existence of the moving image can be summarised and defined as follows: a Model Image is the summation of all the optical illusions presented to a paying audience at any time, in such a way that each viewer can perceive them in their totality.

XX

The spectator tormented

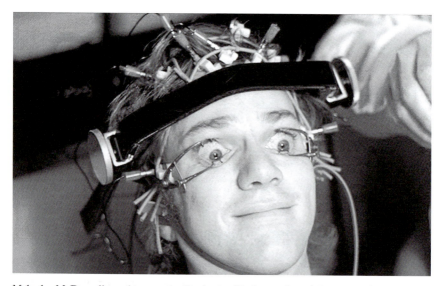

Malcolm McDowell is subject to the 'Ludovico Technique' in *A Clockwork Orange* (Stanley Kubrick, 01971) by being forced to watch a sequence of projected moving images depicting violent events. In the film, a physician humidifies his cornea with an aqueous solution to substitute for the action normally performed by the eyelids. As much a social satire, *A Clockwork Orange* is also a parable on the 'excess' of vision. Watching objects as long as possible without blinking has been a frequent experiment in the history of science, and a number of distinguished astronomers lost their sight after prolonged observation of the sun; Galileo Galilei (01564–01642) was blind during the last four years of his life, probably after peering at the sun through his telescope.

Viewers of the Model Image are unaware of the crisis or catastrophe that will shatter their trust in its integrity. Such an idyllic state is a condition for the existence of this image. As soon as history comes into play, there can still be a relative degree of bliss in watching the image, yet sooner or later some spectators will be able to foresee the rate and patterns of its destruction. (This is impossible in the preceding phase, as they are conscious of nothing but the Model Image.) Film history can predict what the outcome of such a process will be, but in a very limited way only. In a way, indeed, so limited that the accuracy of its predictions is close to nil. It is rather difficult to assess what the consequences may be of the disintegration of the moving image in the mere span of a century. To do it even in the time frame of a decade may be beyond the capacity of human intelligence. It is recognised that the moving image will dissolve sooner or later, yet there is no way of predicting the amount of destruction that will occur in the immediate future. On the other hand, it is quite possible to establish a forecast coefficient based on the spectator's awareness that the object to be viewed represents a balance between costs (of the materials originally used in its manufacture and the space available to view it in) and the opportunity to view it at all. When the coefficient equals zero, it can be said that the viewer is blind (Homer) or has been blinded; or, at the opposite end of the spectrum, that a moving image was forcibly presented to spectators in such a way as to deny them the pleasures of collective distraction – that is, by actions complementary to [XXIII] and compatible with the experience of viewing images that move and speak – or even by being prevented from blinking (Alexander De Large). Given the same number of viewers, as soon as our coefficient rises to 1, each of them would have the capacity to consider the existence of a Model Image as a hypothetical reality. It is also possible, of course, that our spectators are perfectly conscious of watching images that will presently be lost, but consider it irrelevant: *deteriora sequitur*.

XXI
Description of the Model Image according to the chronicles

Cinema Cecchini, Udine, ca. 01935. La Cineteca del Friuli, Gemona/Mario Quargnolo Collection.

According to that view, a Model Image was an original and unrepeatable entity. 'No such thing as two identical viewings. Films sometimes as brief as the twinkling of an eye. Programs of shorts continuously shown. Spectators indifferent to where the cycle begins or ends. Audiences who happily cheer, stomp, eat and make love in front of the screen! Projectionists who arbitrarily slow down or accelerate the speed of reality! Images that appear and vanish even before barkers can describe them. Oxyetheric lamps that hiss in the dark.'

XXII
The Model Image formally defined

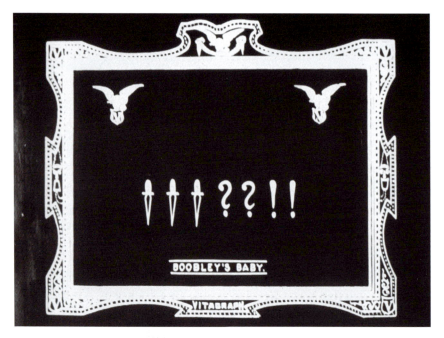

Boobley's Baby (Sidney Drew, Vitagraph, 01915). Frame enlargement from a 35mm acetate print. Library of Congress.

Let t be the running time of a moving image after a number n (wherein $n{\geq}1$) of screenings through an apparatus that inflicts damage on the image such as described in [IV]; let p be the quantity of moving images eliminated from t in order to increase the potential number of viewings; let c be the amount of moving imagery suppressed for cultural reasons; let h be the coefficient of humidity in the viewer's cornea that induces periodic blinking. The Model Image assumes the existence of an ideal running time T, from which are to be subtracted fragments of time derived from h (though sometimes from p) at the very first appearance of the moving image, whose n viewings – which in turn are subjected to the restrictions forced upon c by the accidents of distribution practices – increasingly prevent the viewer from a complete experience of the narrative and the pictorial character of the moving image. (Further variables such as the integrating, deleting or modifying of other features of the Model Image – monochrome duplication of images originally made in colour or vice versa, concealing or removing some portions of the image, the transference of sound into different formats – are not considered in this context, as they do not affect the transition from the ideal time T to the empirical time t. The same applies to the kind of transformation pointed out in [XLVIII], as it is the consequence of an intention to delay or prevent it altogether and therefore subsequent to the definition suggested here.) Needless to say, the existence of T presupposes a viewer placed of his own volition [XIX] before a moving image completed though never seen before, minus all possibility of distraction (such as physical contact with a loved one, a noisy audience, dozing in and out of sleep). Finally, it must be assumed that the moving image is so brief that even a blink of the human eyelid cannot interfere with its full experience (a possibility already considered in [XXI]). As the above conditions are unlikely to occur in the real world all at the same time, then T itself must be regarded as a fictional entity. Which demonstrates that no viewer can claim to have seen a moving image in its entirety.

XXIII
First method to be employed in moving image history

Phenakistoscope disc, 01833. George Eastman House.

No history of cinema can be established without confronting the issues of the physiology and the psychology of perception. Hence, its proper development would be linked to a viewer able to perceive a sequence of moving images that are intact and strike the eye at regular intervals, a viewer who is placed before an entity that appears at a given time but which may be displayed (within certain limits) independent of the presence of spectators, and whose attention span [XXV] is sufficient for the task. It is therefore possible to conceive the following elementary model of the moving image experience: a spectator, whether alone or otherwise isolated from distraction, in a situation wherein the value of h is irrelevant in relation to the time necessary for the display of the images, at an appropriate distance from the screen or other viewing device, in a perfectly designed environment in which the moving image is to be seen, at a time when the spectator is capable of a maximum degree of attention and the variables c and p, as defined in [XXII], have a value equal to nil. It is expected that a time will come when the loneliness of the spectator will be detrimental to the pleasure of experiencing moving images. The terms of the contemplative process will then be subject to a crucial shift and be affected by further variables [XXV].

XXIV
Distraction

'Doctor Mitchoff just made a surprising discovery that allows him to fix in the eye of the dead the features of the last person he laid eyes upon. The scientist submits his discovery to superintendent of police Lenoir, which is of such great consequence to the police, and which shall from now on, in matters of crime, give them irrefutable proof of guilt. Indeed, someone calls from the police station that a crime has just been committed. This provides an opportunity to test the new method on the victim, the usurer Nathan Gobsek. The experiment is a success. Little by little, an image is drawn on the eye. But, the clearer the image, the more the eyes of the superintendent are filled with terror. Soon he can no longer doubt the facts: those are the features of his son etched on the retina of the corpse. After the son has confessed to his poor father that his gambling debts drove him to the crime, the father, holding out a revolver, indicates to him the only choice he has left and the guilty son commits suicide.' Advertising poster for *La Découverte du docteur Mitchoff* (Pathé, 01912), offset lithograph. Source unknown. Plot description is taken from the *Bulletin Pathé* no. 6 (Paris: Pathé, 01912), cat. no. 4897.

Certain actions undertaken by the spectator at the margins of his main activity will subtract several temporal units from the global time T occupied by the Model Image. These actions are often considered necessary complements to the viewing experience. Indeed, in some cases they will take precedence over the act of seeing, thus shunting the image to the background or redefining it as a pretext for other activities [XXI]. The existence of places specifically designed for viewing moving images thus emerges as a catalyst for the performance of a collective ritual [XXVI]. Whenever the quantity of moving images available to a given community exceeds the actual or presumed need (aesthetic or otherwise) for their consumption, and the community endorses the display of non-discrete images – that is, images that form and vanish without being seen in their entirety – there would then be another kind of Model Image, one displayed through electronic or other non-photographic means. In such a case, however, it can be said that a primary source of pleasure, as defined by the viewer's attention to the moving images or to other events connected with its display, has been replaced by another quality of perception. The ideal time T is now deprived of that amount of time no longer determined by the decay of the image carrier [IV] and no longer influenced by a decision to compress different levels of visual, aural or tactile attention [XX] into a single event, but governed instead by an impulse to ignore altogether the process of formation of the image itself.

XXV
Attention

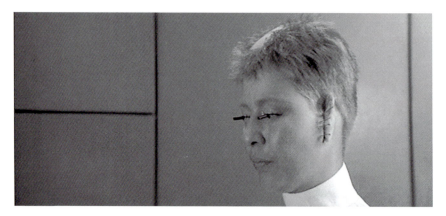

The first known ocular surgeon is an Indian physician called Susruta (ca. 00500 BC). His operating procedure, known as 'couching', consisted in depressing clouded lenses into the vitreous cavity. Twenty-five hundred years later, in *Dune* (David Lynch, 01984), eye prosthetics have become a metaphor of authoritarian society: while being subject to a medical treatment, tyrant Baron Harkonnen is assisted by a physician with optical needles replacing the organs of vision.

As much as it can be explained on economic grounds, the shift to a distracted perception of moving images (its 'inevitability' in face of the electronic image as opposed to its collective function at the cinema: socialising, forming a sense of community, satisfying an imaginary or promised sexual fulfilment) is best understood through a psychological inquiry into the opposite phenomenon. In fact, both viewpoints recognise a common impulse of the image maker to capture, organise and direct the viewer's attention.

XXVI

Wherein film history is finally established

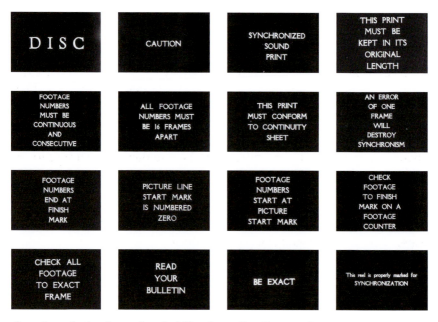

Countdown leader for unidentified Vitaphone film. Frame enlargement from a 35mm acetate print. George Eastman House.

In order to become the object of film history, perceived moving images must also be interpreted in relation to the physical [XXI] and psychological [XXIII] conditions surrounding their appearance. In fact, spectators are bound to perform their role within a context they themselves authorise and endorse, one in which they demand to be entertained according to the expectations (length of the film, day and time of its exhibition), the practices and the customs that accrue to it (a hall where moving images are displayed, a flat or curved screen, a sound system) established by the experience of those who have preceded them.

XXVII
Cinema not an art of reproduction

Tragödie einer Uraufführung (O. F. Maurer, 01926). Frame enlargement from a 35mm acetate print. Film Museum Berlin.

The assumption is that the spectator is indifferent to the fact that the moving image is derived from a matrix, and believes in the possibility of seeing it again under the same conditions as previously. From that standpoint, as much as in oral literature [VI], cinema is not based on reproduction. It is an art of repetition.

XXVIII
Repetition as a catalyst of change

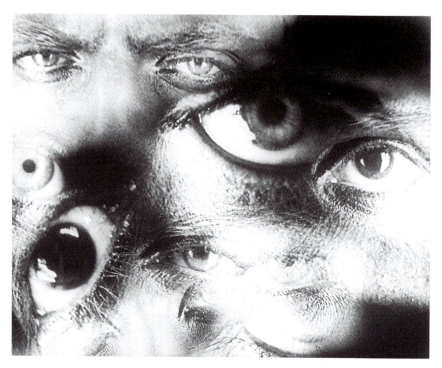

Metropolis (Fritz Lang, 01927). Frame enlargement from a 35mm acetate print. George Eastman House.

This establishes a direct link between the ephemeral nature of the image [IV] and its exhibition in a number n of showings (wherein $n \geq 1$) mistakenly perceived by the viewer as events which are identical to each other [XXVII]. Such definition holds true both for the moving image and for the emission of sounds associated with its display.

XXIX
Evolutionary patterns in the representation of movement

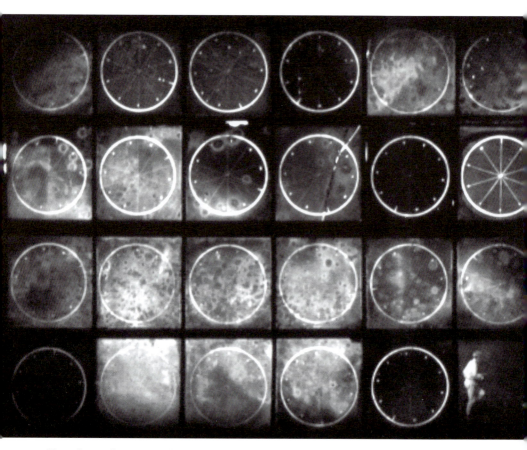

Glass plate with sequence showing a rotating sulky wheel, used to determine the length of time between exposures in Eadweard Muybridge's photographic experiments (May 10, 01885). George Eastman House.

NON-PHOTOMECHANICAL MOVING IMAGES

CINEMA

OPTICAL ILLUSIONS

PAINTINGS

SCULPTURES

BUILDINGS

XXX
Objects of memory

Salò o le centoventi giornate di Sodoma (Pier Paolo Pasolini, 01975).

Travel, leisure, hilarious or notable occurrences are at the origins of the moving image. More precisely, moving images arise out of an intent to transform into an object whatever is forgettable and therefore doomed to decay and oblivion. The impermanence of these events finds its empirical counterpart in the moving image and determines its status as an artifact.

XXXI
The human being as a consumer of images

In February, 01954, the Chaplin Studio on La Brea Boulevard in Hollywood was handed over to its new owners, who planned to outfit it for TV production. The faithful Rollie Totheroh had shipped many negatives and prints over to Switzerland, but much still remained. The new owners threw out the contents of the prop room, where, among hundreds of other items, the giant wooden gears from *Modern Times* (01936) were stored, and they emptied out the film vaults, where the outtakes from nearly forty years were stored. Some of the material was saved by Raymond Rohauer and used by Kevin Brownlow and David Gill in their documentary *Unknown Chaplin* (01983); some was not. In the background stands the house that Chaplin built on the property for his brother Sydney. A grocery store now stands on that spot. Scott Eyman Collection.

When moving images were first experienced, human beings feasted on visions of extremely short duration, more or less equal to the attention span that could be assigned to an event whose very existence was in itself a surprise [XXI]. For a brief period, such a duration (corresponding to a limited number of times t along a clearly defined time frame) had to be considered as constant. However, these moving images, apparently thought of as durable [XXVII] even while experienced in the course of being progressively dissolved, were repeatedly shown in different locations and at different times until they were completely destroyed at last – that is, when the physical condition of the carrier was in a state so disastrous as to make its further exhibition virtually impossible. These moving images, therefore, had a fate similar to that of other ephemeral forms of expression such as operetta and the various Universal Expositions. Exploited to the utmost, their carriers had no further reason to exist; their destruction was not only inevitable but desirable insofar as new carriers and new images had to be created for commercial reasons [XIX]. Despite all the claims to justify it in the light of a given cultural programme, any attempt to restore the moving image derives from motivations which are at best alien, if not contrary, to the unstable nature of the carrier. The main aim of each project of preservation of the moving image is therefore, *strictu sensu*, an impossible attempt to stabilise a thing that is inherently subject to endless mutation and irreversible destruction. Trying to impose a reversal of this process (a goal incoherent in itself, as no reconstruction of the moving image can be accomplished without trying to imagine what the Model Image looked like, thus separating it still further from a previous character which itself is unknown to the preservationist) is tantamount to a denial that the moving image has a history. On the contrary, becoming part of the process and accepting it as the workings of a natural phenomenon is to recognise the nature of the Model Image and to cultivate an intelligent awareness that each showing will hasten its demise [L]. Conceived in those terms, the effort to preserve a moving image in the state in which it was found (plus making it viewable to others, once the loss of information deriving from the process has been acknowledged) has at least some chance of being useful by fostering the concept of durability, its potential and its limitations. A vain effort it is, but also one that is fertile in its implications. Preservation of the moving image is a necessary mistake.

XXXII
The iconoclasts (continued)

Taliban students burning films in Kabul, Afghanistan. BBC broadcast, October 15, 01996.

The confluence of a variety of elements leading to the destruction of the moving image is also the outcome of climactic and geographic components. In addition to what has been mentioned in [I] concerning communities with no sense of moving image history, one must add those deriving from adverse environmental conditions such as are referred to in [IV]. Given these circumstances, each historical period is characterised by societies in which the creation of moving images is encouraged, and by other societies that regard them with such ignorance and fear as to result in mistreatment that hastens their demise and radically modifies the patterns of periodisation described in [IX].

XXXIII
No such thing as a Golden Age of the moving image

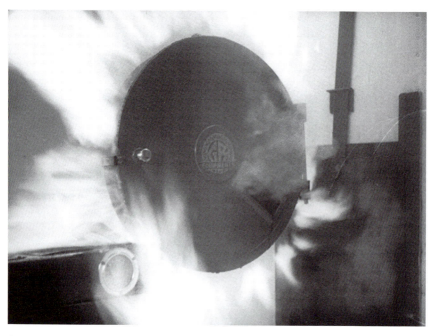

This Film Is Dangerous (Ronald Haines, British Documentary Films, 01948) describes the effects of a nitrate fire in a projection booth. In another educational film on the same subject, *Das Verhalten von brennendem Nitrofilm gegenüber löschmitteln* (Österreichisches Filmarchiv, 01978), a fire squad demonstrates various unsuccessful attempts at putting out burning reels of nitrate stock in the outskirts of Vienna. In hindsight, this is the snuff movie of cinema itself – people gathering in order to destroy moving images and see how fast they can burn. The frame enlargement reproduced above is taken from a 35mm acetate print at the Film and Video Archive, Imperial War Museum, London, courtesy of Roger Smither.

A Golden Age of the moving image – that is, its existence in a timeless state of stability – would be possible only if films had never been run through projectors, or if matrices had never been used for their duplication into prints. Such a Golden Age would be rendered still more impossible by the matrix itself being subject to a process of degradation that is identical to the decay of the images produced by it.

XXXIV
Creativity and the consumption of images

A cyclops character in *X-Men* (Bryan Singer, 02000) brings the *Odyssey* to the realm of science fiction. Contrary to common belief, the inability to perceive the depth of field does not affect only those who see things through a single eye. Studies in ophtalmology have revealed that a surprisingly high percentage of viewers cannot actually experience depth of field, thus being unable, for example, to observe it in a 3-D film. The fluorescent eyes of some of the mutants in *X-Men* confirm an axiom of modern mythology, according to which the superiority of artificial intelligence is most often symbolised by their viewing apparatus.

Periodisation in film history [IX] is the product of an estimate in which the rate of absorption of moving images is compared with the coefficient of loss or decay of images previously made, in addition to the relationship obtaining between the above coefficients and the technology designed to produce these images. For each given group of spectators it is possible to establish a rate of consumption of moving images and a rate of creativity corresponding to the ability of the image maker to meet the viewer's expectations for surprise [XXXI] and attention [XXV]. Implicit in this is the understanding that these rates are dependent on the permanence and flexibility of the technique adopted for the purpose, and its cost.

XXXV
Compulsory solutions

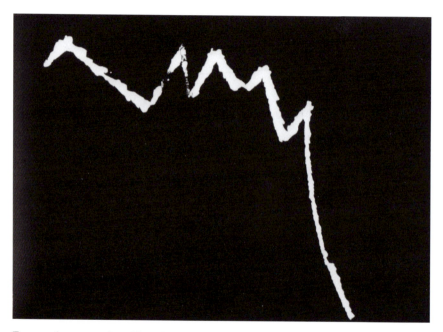

Frame enlargement from New Zealand experimental film-maker Len Lye's *Free Radicals* (US, 01958/01979) in which Lye scratched 'white ziggle-zag-splutter scratches' directly onto black 16mm leader. Courtesy of the Len Lye Foundation, New Zealand.

The rate of creativity suggested in [XXXIV] is not directly proportional to the complexity of the techniques needed to produce moving images. According to a common paradox of human experience, the quest for new ideas is often encouraged as much by indigence as by prosperity.

XXXVI
Law of equilibrium

A machine for shredding 35mm feature films after their commercial distribution. The equipment, known as 'the guillotine' and located in Cinisello Balsamo near Milan, Italy, shreds 150,000 prints of polyester film per year, coming from all over Europe. The material is converted into low-cost fuel for industrial plants and raw material for benches, combs, eyeglass frames and clothing. A similar plant in Millesimo, also in Italy, is dedicated to the recycling of triacetate cellulose film. *Due dollari al chilo* (Paolo Lipari, 02000). Frame enlargement by Paolo Jacob from a 35mm polyester print. Fondazione Cineteca Italiana, Milano.

The study of the chemical factors and the commercial and cultural circumstances leading to the disappearance of moving images shows that the visual memory of a society tends to constellate in accordance with a coefficient of multiplication (of whatever the viewer expects to see, and of the techniques for the purpose of meeting such expectations) and a coefficient of limitation. The value of the latter is given by the variables described in [IV] and the highest number of moving images that can be identified, catalogued and viewed [XLIV] in a given time span; beyond that number there is nothing but pointless accumulation, a waste of energy directed towards the intellectual control of a corpus far too huge to be grasped; the syndrome of the Universal Filmography. This law of equilibrium applies itself with ease to the photographic moving image, whose loss is the outcome of clearly defined causes [IV]. It is somewhat less so in the case of the electronic and digital image, by virtue of the infinite fragmentation of an endless number of events, a number so vast that the attempt to assess what is worth seeing and what may be allowed to disappear becomes itself a hopeless task.

XXXVII
The principle of inertia

The close-up of Norman Bates watching Marion Crane through a hole in the wall has become an icon of voyeurism and vision as a transgressive event. Four decades after *Psycho* (01960), Norman Bates experiences *déjà vu* in the ultimate remake (01998) of Alfred Hitchcock's classic. Director Gus Van Sant adhered to a self-imposed rule of constraint by using the same score and screenplay of the earlier version. However, there are several deviations from the original; a particularly striking example is the detail of Marion's dilating pupil as she is stabbed in the shower.

The possibility cannot be ruled out that the vanishing of the electronic and digital image in the viewer's memory [XXIV] could be due to the relative simplicity of using a complex technology and its effects on the level of attention [XXV], not to mention the incomplete nature of the image itself. Such an attention level can be estimated by subtracting the element of surprise described in [XXXI] from the viewer's impulse to come to rest in front of a moving image. The same precept of inertia enables the viewer to tolerate patterns of narration and perception evolving at an extremely slow rate and progressively diluted in time, the cultural equivalent of the second principle of thermodynamics.

XXXVIII
The pornographic image

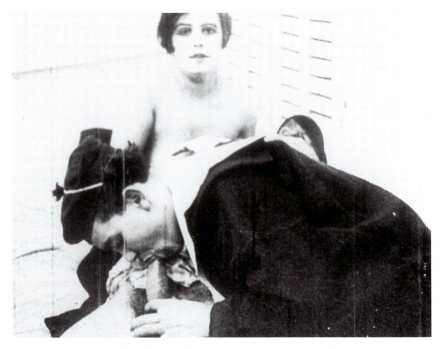

Cast Ashore (Producer unknown, US, ca. 01920), one of the earliest pornographic films to feature gay sex. Frame enlargement from a 35mm nitrate print. George Eastman House.

In establishing itself as a theoretical entity, the Model Image finds its counterpart in the pornographic image. Its statutory component is so-called 'vice', that is, the gap between sexuality and purposeful human reproduction. The spectator contemplating such imagery is accorded a privileged status, in the sense that the time t is supposed to be equal to the actual or presumed duration of the sexual acts represented in it. The (typically) secretive function of these images brings the viewer to a maximum degree of attention [XXV] towards bodies and objects exhibited in a time frame that is not far from real experience (hence their relative inattention to aesthetic forms) in view of actual or imagined repetition of desired events such as masturbation or coitus. However, the conditions under which these images are made and presented, the objections raised against their collective consumption [XXIV] – often circumvented altogether through devices aimed at satisfying the urge of solitary viewing – and the social stigma attached to them guarantees that the corpus of moving images pertaining to the need to address or fulfill the above practices is not generally considered as part of film history in the common sense of the term [II]. Indeed, by the standards of that history the pornographic image does not exist at all. The lack of recognised artistic value – a variable already described in [VI] – and the fact that such imagery is intended to flaunt the moral codes generally accepted in public life, make its destruction an occurrence not merely inevitable, but one that is quite taken for granted. While the Model Image is the abstract of unachieved possibility, its opposite is one that should have never seen the light in the first place.

XXXIX
Is film history monotonous?

The Falls (Peter Greenaway, 01980). British Film Institute.

It ought to be. As long as cinema is an art of repetition [XXVII] based on imperceptible deviations from the norm of previously established canons [XXXVII], its history will be concerned with mutations affecting the physical evidence of the image rather than with any evolution [XXIX] in the expression of meanings (such meanings being superficially altered by technological advance and the search for unusual narrative patterns: Tulse Luper). The monotony of cinema has also a rhythmic quality, in that the retina is stimulated by complete images at regular intervals [XXIII]. Other systems for the creation of artificial visions [XXIV] involve a continuous display of incomplete images, presented to the viewer in the very act of formation. To speak of a Model Image in relation to its non-discrete (electronic or whatever) form is a contradiction in terms.

XL
Imaginary colours

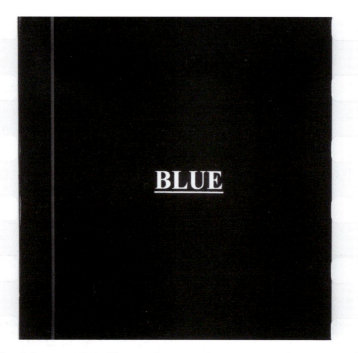

Blue (Derek Jarman, 01993). Frame enlargement from a 35mm polyester print. George Eastman House. Courtesy James Mackay, Basilisk Communications.

As with the Model Image, its colour is a mythical entity, a construct of the mind. Therefore the question of its instability and transformation in time applies both to the image carrier and the viewer. From that perspective, the analysis of moving images does not greatly differ from the study of paintings, sculptures, miniatures and crafts. Once again, the difference lies in chronological patterns of decay, their scope, and a perception of their progress [IX]; anything that can be inferred from it is the outcome of an uneven mediation between memory (what has been seen) and experience (what is being seen, here and now). Colour fading can be accepted as the result of a flawed technology [XXXIX] or challenged through imperfect renewal or restoration of its presumed qualities, but neither response justifies establishing a code of aesthetic values derived from it. If the object to be analysed is not the evidence – be it ever so deceptive – of a visual phenomenon but rather its simulation in the form of a reproduction (in itself the reflection of a current technique or taste), then making meaning of it is, at best, a fascinating yet empty exercise, at worst, another kind of ideology: false consciousness, false representation.

XLI
Monsters

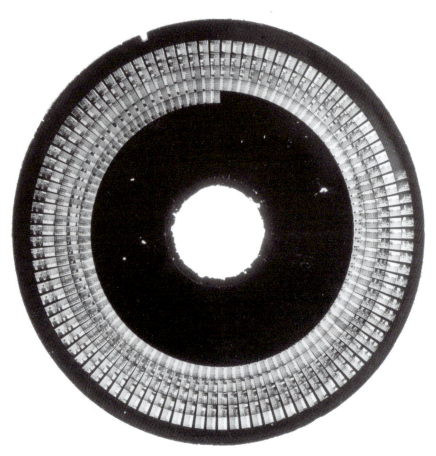

Leonard Ulrich Kamm, Kammatograph, 01898–01900. Unidentified film [*Street scene*]. Glass plate (actual diameter, 30.5cm) with ca. 550 frames (8.4 x 6mm). George Eastman House.

In the chronicles of the moving image, novelty is represented by visual events produced with anomalous techniques. Such is the case of film on glass, aimed at preventing the untimely destruction of the carrier due to ignition; the mirages presented to wild animals in order to study their reactions; the Braille film, which was supposed to provide the visually impaired with a tactile surface for mental images as a surrogate for those projected onto a screen. The same applies to cinema experienced through other technologies, or to the electronic and digital image transferred onto photographic film. These hybrids announce a coming change, not in the content of the moving image or in the way it is organised into concepts and narrative patterns [XXXIX], but in the processes and rate of its loss – yet another shift in the modes of perceiving artificial reality.

XLII
The ultimate goal of film history

Advertising poster for *Das Ende* (Deutsche Mutoscop- u. Biograph GmbH, Germany, 01912). From *Filmplakate 1908–1932. Aus den beständen des Staatlichen Filmarchivs der DDR* (Potsdam: Ausstellung im Filmmuseum der DDR, 01986), p. 48.

The ultimate goal of film history is an account of its own disappearance, or its transformation into another entity. In such a case, a narrating presence has the prerogative of resorting to the imagination to describe the phases leading from the hypothetical Model Image to the complete oblivion of what the moving image once represented.

XLIII
The film historian must be a storyteller

Intertitle from an unidentified Mack Sennett comedy, ca. 01920. Cineteca del Friuli/ David H. Shepard.

Film history comes to exist as such when moving image destruction is described and explained in order to make clear the causes and patterns of decay of the Model Image. Contrary to the formal approach outlined in [XXII], such description is affected by so many unforeseeable factors that the language of the exact sciences is inadequate for the purpose. On the other hand, film history is quite compatible with a narrating presence [XLII] and with the goal of deciphering the traces left by each viewing on the relics of an entity recognised as being no longer extant. The imaginary object will then be mirrored in an imaginary account: an exercise in story-telling.

XLIV
The unseen

Waiting room of the dormitory at Oregon State University, Corvalis, Oregon, ca. 01966 (*Alfred Hitchcock Presents*). Photo by Ken Deroux. Courtesy of Edith Kramer.

Relatively few moving images can be seen in the course of a lifetime, a tiny fraction of those actually made. Given an average lifespan of seventy-five years, the time spent viewing them rarely exceeds one hundred thousand hours, little more than a decade. Those who live in communities where moving images are made and experienced on a regular basis sometimes have an urge to watch as many of them as possible [XXXIV]. This urge is often replaced by other impulses such as boredom, selectivity, or flat refusal. The death of cinema is primarily a mental phenomenon that will occur whether or not the factors mentioned in [IV] actually take place, and will be sanctioned by the natural tendency to forget the experience of pleasure. The search for its repetition, as represented by the practices referred to in [XXVII], is also typical of humans.

XLV
The subjective image

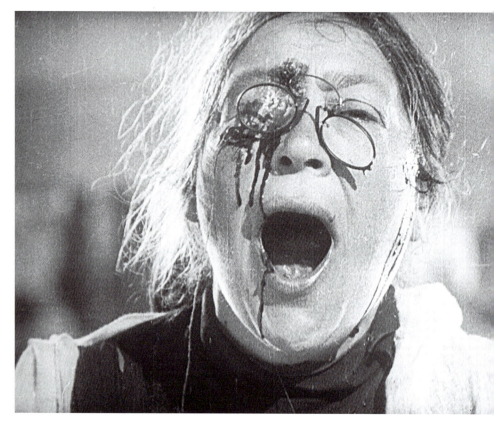

Bronenosets Potyomkin [Battleship Potemkin] (Sergei M. Eisenstein, 01925). Frame enlargement from a 35mm acetate print. George Eastman House.

Which refers to all the images that are corrupted by the viewer, even as they are regarded as pristine [XX]. Images of great value to some spectators and quite irrelevant to others [VI]. Images experienced too early in life (due to distraction [XXIV], ignorance [XV] or innocence [XXI]). Images seen too many times or too late in life, when curiosity [XLIV] has been exhausted or jaded by experiences occurring before the viewing has taken place.

XLVI
Distant views

Hēnare Tahiwi and Ellen Te Wānui Knocks Cook, both of Ngati Raukawa iwi Ngati Maiotaki hapu. *Historic Ōtaki, Tangi and Funeral of Te Rauparaha's Niece, Heeni Te Rei* (01921). Frame enlargement from a 35mm nitrate print. Courtesy Raukawa Trustees and The New Zealand Film Archive/Ngā Kaitiaki O Ngā Taonga Whitiāhua.

We know little or nothing about the moving images produced in remote parts of the world and lost soon after their first exhibition. What kind of images can be seen in Baku? What is available to a viewer in Taveuni? What do they make of our images? Their relative distance leaves us with the same lack of involvement we feel at the news of the passing away of a person we have never heard of before.

XLVII
Why do humans want to see things again?

Peeping Tom (Michael Powell, 01960) has been described as the first commercial feature film dealing with the phenomenon of 'snuff movies'. This might explain the outraged reactions to Powell's last film at the time of its release: 'the sickest and filthiest film I remember seeing' (Isobel Quigley in the *Guardian*). 'The only really satisfactory way to dispose of *Peeping Tom* would be to shovel it up and flush it swiftly down the nearest sewer. Even then, the stench would remain' (Derek Hill, *Tribune*); 'wholly evil' (Nina Hibbin, the *Daily Worker*). Ten years later, unverified reports from the United States and South America referred to the production of amateur films allegedly showing the actual torture, mutilation and killing of people. An investigation conducted by the FBI in 01971 failed to ascertain the extent to which these films were in fact circulating in the underground market.

Three motivations are certain: the pleasure of repeating an experience of pleasure [XLIV]. A desire to obtain a fuller perception of what has already been seen. A change of opinion. Another catalyst — realising that one has failed to see or was noticing the wrong things the first time — may sometimes appear after a further viewing has taken place for spectators endowed with the faculty of introspection.

XLVIII
The role of fiction in moving image preservation

Leonard Zelig stands between US president Herbert Hoover (right) and Calvin Coolidge in *Zelig* (Woody Allen, 01980), a landmark pseudo-documentary on fake, celebrity, and image manipulation. When the creators of *Toy Story* (John Lasseter, 01995) went to make a DVD version of the film, twelve percent of the digital masters had already vanished. For three months, Pixar Animation Studios staff scoured the system for the toys' missing parts – salvaging all but one percent of what had been lost in the computers. The remaining scenes were reassembled. For subsequent Pixar movies, Lasseter said, 'we have a better backup system'. Digital technology was still in its infancy when *Zelig* was made, but the issues raised by Allen's fictional biography have been confirmed by the collapse of photography as a document of the empirical world.

The intention of bringing the moving image back to its supposed primordial state leads to the creation of fictive artifacts. Such a proceeding has the effect of widening the gap between the image as it is and its hypothetical condition as a Model Image. Strictly speaking, the effects of doing so are identical to the damage already suffered by the object being looked at [XXXI]. Giving up the attempt altogether or opposing it, on the other hand, is to fall prey to the illusion that the moving image can be frozen in time, as if it could no longer be affected by history. The formal definition [XXII] should therefore include a variable r for restoration, to account for the drifting of the original viewing event into a fiction [XLIII]. The notion of an 'authentic' restoration is a cultural oxymoron.

XLIX
Model Image and music performance

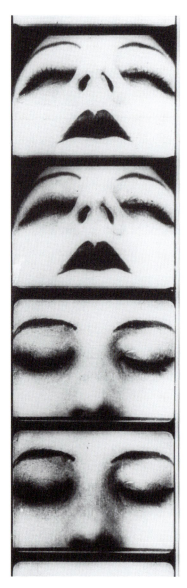

Ballet mécanique (Fernand Léger and Dudley Murphy, 01924). British Film Institute.

Any endeavour to protect the moving image from the environmental [IV] and psychological [XLIV] factors leading to its decay is doomed to failure [XXXI] as long as the viewing experience is conceived of as an event that can be repeated indefinitely [XXVII]. The nature of the light source, the apparatus, the physical structure of the image carrier [IV] and the architectural space in which the event occurs are variables which have the power to determine the quality of visual perception and its patterns. Given their huge number, each with its vast potential for mutation [XLIII], preservation of the moving image ought to be treated as an equivalent to musical performance. As with the moving image, each aural experience is in fact a unique event; both are subject to variations due to their transfer to another object (musical score and matrix), their display (concert and screening), their repetition (sound recording and viewing print).

L
Towards an ethics of vision

A group of executives throwing away Goldberg shipping cans for 35mm film. The symbolic event took place at a press conference announcing the conversion to digital of the AMC Empire 25 Cinema in Times Square 2000, New York City, and was reported by the *New York Times* on November 26, 02000. Photo courtesy of Paul Pinner, Boeing Company.

The proposed solution [XLIX] to the dilemma referred to in [XXXI] is at best incomplete, as it does not affect the process of destruction of the Model Image. In this respect, the gap between moving image destruction and the efforts to prevent it is bound to yawn wider than ever. The only alternative possible is a radical change of perspective: giving up all claim to resurrecting the Model Image, as well as all the ambitions underlying the attempt (including the technical term 'restoration', which is a blatant contradiction of the aim). Moving image preservation will then be redefined as the science of its gradual loss and the art of coping with the consequences, very much like a physician who has accepted the inevitability of death even while he continues to fight for the patient's life. In monitoring the progress of image decay, the conservator assumes the responsibility of following the process until the image has vanished altogether, or ensures its migration to another kind of visual experience, while interpreting the meaning of the loss for the benefit of future generations. In doing so, the conservator – no less than the viewer – plays a creative role that is in some way comparable to the work of the image maker. The final outcome of the death of cinema is the foundation of an ethics of vision and the transformation of the Model Image into the Moral Image, mirroring the imperatives and values connected with the act of viewing.

LI
In praise of passivity

The Vampire (Kalem, 01913). George Eastman House.

The guiding principle of the Moral Image is passivity. It entails a relentless effort to minimise any intervention whose aim is to conceal the fact that the moving image has a genetically preordained history and a limited lifespan. Its preservation (a term whose inadequacy has been pointed out in [XLVIII]) would no longer presume to erase history from the body of the image itself. Its procedures would be concerned with implementing all the measures necessary to a respectful control of the processes of decay, serving as an invisible guide through the various ages of the moving image with a vigilant yet unobtrusive attitude toward the indicators of the process (patina, material and narrative gaps, colour fading, sound degradation).

LII
When does posterity end?

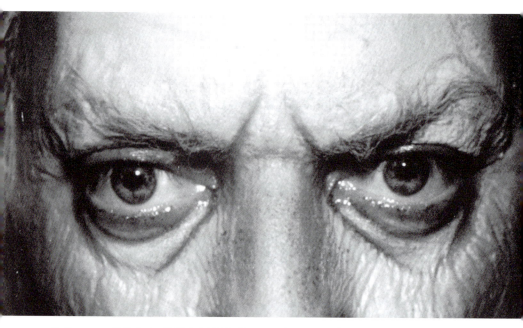

Il Casanova di Federico Fellini (01976). Frame enlargement from a 35mm acetate print. Courtesy of Harvard Film Archive.

The criterion of passivity suggested in [LI] is bound to clash with objections of an economic nature [XIX] on those occasions when the image maker is asked to simulate Model Images of a character determined by the futile yearning for eternity [XXVII]. Hence the need to redefine the principle of the Model Image itself, transposing it out of the domain of theoretical speculation and into the actual viewing experience. It does not matter whether a given method of producing moving images is likely to extend their life expectancy in accordance with the set of cultural values a community of viewers may happen to share. The real question is, are viewers willing to accept the slow fading to nothing of what they are looking at? Is it fair to encourage them to believe that they will never witness the inevitable, and that its actual experience will be left to someone else?

A READER'S REPORT TO THE PUBLISHER

Madam,

I return herewith the manuscript of the work in progress you were good enough to pass along to me. I was already familiar with most of the ideas described in this treatise and if I have disagreements it is not because I find them unacceptable in themselves but because they don't go far enough in addressing what I consider the most important aspect of the matter he attempts to treat, namely, the alarming growth of prejudice against all moving images that exist, or have existed, but which have not been seen.

I won't shed tears over the death of cinema. This might be its first real chance to be taken seriously. It is estimated that about one and a half billion viewing hours of moving images were produced in the year 01999, twice the number made just a decade before. If that rate of growth continues, three billion viewing hours of moving images will be made in 02006, and six billion in 02011. By the year 02025 there will be some one hundred billion hours of these images to be seen. In 01895, the ratio was just above forty minutes, and most of it is now preserved. The meaning is clear. One and a half billion hours is already well beyond the capacity of any single human: it translates into more than 171,000 viewing years of moving pictures in a calendar year. Some may say that a good deal of that figure is produced by video cameras monitoring bank counters and parking lots, but I do not. With or without security monitors, the overall number of moving images we are preserving today is infinitesimal compared with mainstream commercial production. In India alone several hundred films are made a year, and only a tiny portion of them end in the archives. Television in developing countries is produced on videotapes that are erased every few months. If so many of those images come and go without our even hearing about them, then how in the world can we form an idea of what cultural heritage is? The manuscript you are considering shows just the tip of the iceberg of moving image decay, and we miss the true proportions of it by not directing our attention to what lies below the water line. We quake with fear at a collision that has already taken place, and congratulate ourselves that we still have a mission to accomplish. Save our movie heritage! Rescue our history! When in fact we have already scrapped the notion of history, and are doing just fine without it. What I dislike is the pretense that we still have one. The most fictional form of this fantasy is called moving image preservation, a thing promoted by archivists to enhance their own importance. Well, they *are* important, but not for the reasons they imagine. Let me illustrate with an example from my own experience.

Some fifteen years ago, at the end of a meeting with the director of one of the major European film archives, the topic came up of the so-called vinegar syndrome, the irreversible chemical process of decomposition affecting prints struck on cellulose diacetate and triacetate. The issue, I was told, transcended the fact that thousands of the films we thought we had already preserved for posterity were heading for the same kind of decay we had witnessed before they were transferred from nitrate stock. What we thought of as a recent discovery was something chemists had long been familiar with. It was suggested, however, that we not advertise the fact. 'Imagine the impact it would have on our preservation projects. What reaction could you expect from donors and from sources of public funding if they were to learn that the money already invested in preserving our collections will keep them safe for just a short while longer?' In a catchphrase dear to the archivists of the 01970s and reproduced on many of their desks in the form of pop-art badges, Nitrate Won't Wait. Well, Acetate Won't Either.

Much has happened since then, but the vinegar syndrome is more than ever with us to gnaw at our collections, and no remedy will defeat it altogether. The best we can do is to decelerate the process by keeping the films in vaults where temperature and humidity are strictly controlled. Polyester film – which is apparently not subject to the same kind of decay – may or may not be a viable alternative (emulsion likewise carries its own doom, regardless of the base) – but it's worth a try. As it is, we have very little choice in the matter since manufacturers are gradually phasing out the production of acetate and replacing it with polyester, a matter on which they have certainly not asked for our advice. Digital technology offers the seductive promise of a real miracle: perfect vision, eternal moving images that can be reproduced ad infinitum with no loss of visual information – as blatant a lie as the claim that compact discs and cd-roms will last a lifetime. Meanwhile we go on restoring film on film – acetate or polyester: why not nitrate? We spend vast amounts of money trying to improve on the methods of our predecessors, then sit back and hope for the best.

It may interest your author to know that there is no reason to take pride in demonstrating our defeat in such wealth of detail and with such outrageous arrogance. As an antidote to the disease of the ephemeral, he buries the cause of film preservation in the graveyard of which his collection of aphorisms consists. I hope he is satisfied. Has anyone ever been naïve enough to believe that cinema could be preserved like the cave paintings of Lascaux? Did we really fool ourselves into thinking that *Citizen Kane* could be saved for future generations just as we claim to save the Sistine Chapel, Mozart's Jupiter Symphony, the Taj Mahal and Nefertari's jewels? Well, it's not possible, and it never was.

The fact ought to be faced that the most stable medium known to human civilization is not film, whether nitrate cellulose, acetate, or (as far as anyone can tell) polyester. Ceramics can last for millennia. Glass is reasonably safe too. Stone can be affected by climate and pollution. Canvas and wood have problems of their own. Something can be done for paper and frescoes, but gelatine emulsion is a thin layer of organic matter. Gelatine. Animal bones crushed and melted into a semitransparent layer intermixed with crystals of silver salts. It won't last: it can't. Then, what are we to do? Pretend it isn't true? Avoid discussing it? Invoke the digital goddess to spare us the guilty knowledge of impending and irredeemable doom? Or shall we just stand by and reinvent ourselves as caretakers of a monumental necropolis of precious documents, for whom restoration means prolonging their expensive agony?

What person in their right mind would want to perform such a role. Personally, I'd much rather turn my attention to more rewarding activities such as perfume making, sex and landscape gardening. Nostalgia in any form gives me the creeps. Brooding over the past bores me to death, and I pray for the patience to deal with people whose concern for cinema extends no further than knowing who turned the crank, how many films were made, the number of missing frames, who has the most accurate lists, and who is cleverest at organising them. Wake up and look around you! These are just moving shadows! A mere century of history! A hundred years worth of patents, matinees and forgotten celebrities! Other people's leisure time turned into the subject of academic pursuits! In terms of geology, what is a century? Less than nothing. In terms of aesthetics, what is a century? A few pages of a book's chapter, not even that, considering film hasn't gained a place in art history textbooks. Why trouble ourselves? When told that New Zealand was at last going to have its own national film archive, experimental filmmaker Len Lye stared at its newly appointed director and asked, 'Will it foster creativity?'

As far as I can see, there is little real justification for what we do. And I have no patience for a discipline that presumes to instruct me in what art is (the *politique des auteurs*, a lesson in film style, the hundred best movies ever made) or what has value as a document (everything that isn't art: industrial, educational, scientific, promotional, amateur, propaganda films; pornography, B-movies). Documents of what? Of the air, heavy with indifference, that pervades the archives where these images are kept? Of the hypocrisy of governments who tell us a film isn't worth saving unless it's a masterpiece, and then won't give us enough money to save even those? We have made a shelter for millions of reels – anything, whatever we could find – and are now forced to go the other way around and abide by the same laws we have so proudly defied. The tyranny of selection, of choice, of cultural discrimination. Consider it this way. There's a physician, there are ten thousand patients, and there's enough medicine to cure perhaps a hundred. The physician is you. Consult your feelings. Which patients will you choose to treat? And what will you say to the ninety-nine hundred who are denied treatment while they watch the lucky minority exit the hospital? Restoring one, ten, or a hundred films is a symbolic gesture of little consequence, no matter how important the films, unless it is matched by an awareness of the untreated supplicants.

As we discover when we inspect our vaults, nitrate images don't dissolve as quickly as we first believed. Quite the contrary. Some of them will last more than a while, outliving their acetate relatives and perhaps surviving even ourselves. Nitrate indeed often will wait. Which means that with the same amount of money needed to duplicate a hundred nitrate prints we could perhaps preserve twenty times that many in a climatised vault with adequate conditions of temperature and humidity. The estimated life of a print can be doubled just by bringing down the thermostat a few degrees – an interesting bit of news for those who used to insist that nitrate should be destroyed after it's been copied! (Getting rid of the original prints after preservation – officially, for security reasons – was not uncommon till the 01970s, and the massacre is still going on in some countries.) The work of a moving image archive, therefore, is something more than rushing a nitrate print to the lab and getting its reproduction to look as new as possible. The moral to be drawn from this is that at the dawn of an era where the moving picture is gradually suffering the loss of the object that carries it – in this case, the photographic film – the object itself is becoming more valuable than ever. The season of laserdiscs was brief, it's already history. Videotapes will probably last a bit longer by virtue of being cheap and easier to market in developing countries, but their days too are numbered. DVD may or may not set the standard for years to come, but our grandchildren are likely to see it as yet another episode in the archaeology of the motion picture. Consider the history of recorded sound. Phonograph discs running at 78 rpm lasted about half a century. Vinyl long-playing records enjoyed a heyday of thirty years before heading for the flea markets. The compact disc is already ailing after less than two decades. What next? Something new every year, as in the fashion industry? Time will tell, but whatever the next new technological wonder proves to be, the results will be the same. Whatever that may happen to be, you will be told there's no need to keep the old nitrate or acetate junk, because it is all digitised. Later on, they will take back that advice. Or pretend they never gave it; make a B-line to the garbage bin (or to the archive, which has been for them more or less the same thing until recently, but much cheaper than a recycling programme) to sort through the debris for what is salvageable and transferable to another newborn technology – in short, come knocking on our doors in hopes we didn't follow their example or take their advice.

All of which means that an archive for moving images will end as a kind of museum – in the sense we currently give that term of an asylum for cultural artifacts, notwithstanding the tendency to run them like high-class amusement parks. Museums themselves may finally be forced to give a coherent answer to a dilemma they have been living with for decades. Are they to be archives in the literal sense, or venues for permanent theme festivals? Are they to preserve or to show? The most logical course would be to separate those functions altogether: care for the artifacts in one place, and in another (close enough to the archive) develop strategies for intellectual access, but since when do developments follow a logical pattern? It is difficult enough to explain the need for the maintenance of collections and to attract funding for that purpose – especially when there is little more to show than a frosted storage room. Showing on a big screen what has been collected is no less important, but it requires the attention and the interest of the public, and the public is seldom enough willing to let the archives have their say.

What happens when there is a collision between the interests of the programmer of festivals and those of the collection manager (as the Artist formerly known as Curator is now called)? To dramatise the point, let us imagine that a consortium of archives of the moving image has undertaken a new reconstruction of what we shall call *The Absolute Masterpiece*® (Restoration™ No. 456 ©), directed sometime during the 01920s by an Undisputed Genius of Cinema. Let us also assume that the film has been available for decades. And incidentally, wasn't there another highly touted restoration of the same film just a few years ago? Yes, but some newly discovered footage may bring us closer to the look the film had in the 01920s. In that case, good! Besides, because of recent improvements in laboratory techniques, we can now be sure that the images will be sharper than ever. In that case, very good! It also seems that an incomplete nitrate negative of a foreign language version has come to light. In that case, excellent! And besides, some tinted prints were unearthed a few years ago, and it may now be possible to inject some colour into the preservation copies. In that case, splendid! There's even an annotated script, censorship documents, and a complete set of previously unpublished production stills. In that case, what are we waiting for? Let us by all means restore *The Absolute Masterpiece*® for the upteenth time. There are so many reasons why we should. A fellow institution outside the consortium, the Faraway Film Archive, has also preserved a complete first generation print of another foreign language version of it, whose footage could be helpful in bringing *The Absolute Masterpiece*® back in all its pristine glory. For surely no restoration is pointless as long as it does the job better than it's ever been done before. Yet to what degree does that remain true? Will the time ever come when we leave *The Absolute Masterpiece*® alone for a while and concentrate on some of the catastrophes that are staring us in the face?

A ghost haunts the corridors of the film archives, the ghost of redundant restoration, otherwise known as new restoration. Its presence is hardly unexpected, yet it has now reached alarming proportions, affecting as it does all institutions whose *raison d'être* is the preservation of the moving image. The rationale behind the phenomenon of the archival remake is complex and often contradictory, but here are some of its recurring themes.

1) Audiences are eager to see these films. Collectors would like to own them in the form of viewing copies, whether photomechanic or digital. Before anything else, archivists would like to extend them their protection. But not long after it had established itself as an art and a technique, film preservation began to take on the features of a business operation. Ambitious terms such as 'restored', 'reconstructed', or 'digitally remastered' are at times quite misleadingly used by corporate entities, by festivals, and even a by boisterous minority of film archives in order to promote unpublicised agendas of their own, in which case it would be wise to take their testimony with a grain of salt. Given a negative or a print in good shape plus a sufficiency of funds, it's all packed up and sent to the lab, where the trick is swiftly performed. In some cases all that has happened is a clean-up of the negative and the addition of some colour saturation to give it a brighter look. Which is not exactly a restoration. However, you are forbidden to say so because they not you are the specialists, the prints you saw were scratched and faded, and you obviously don't remember how bad they looked, so hold your tongue and pay close attention to the words of wisdom that are emanating from their publicity departments. Production companies – the very same which till 01960 were unfazed by the prospect of losing their older negatives through ruin because they supposed there was no more money to be made out of them – are largely responsible for

this, though they are now aware that with just a little effort certain of these old films may be turned into breadwinners again.

2) The public and private institutions who finance restoration projects are often motivated by a desire for prestige that renders them indifferent to the fate of thousands of interesting but totally unprestigious titles that will never attract the attention of mass audiences. (Sales of the average video release of a silent film in the United States rarely exceed 1500 copies.) The price to be paid for the dictatorship of public opinion is legitimate when it promotes film preservation as a cause worthy in itself rather than a mere luxury for a privileged élite. But in some countries there is a perverse disposition to 'restore' films which are already preserved elsewhere. There is something downright immoral about a duplication of effort upon a classic for no other reason than to assert a claim to prominence in the field, when a hundred films of unknown origin but of real interest are left to rot in the vaults.

3) After years of ransacking their holdings, the archives have few lost masterworks left to rediscover. A gem here and there perhaps, but they get rarer all the time. Gone is the golden age of the triumphant reemergence of the 'lost' film, an age that owed so much to the initiatives of institutions like the Nederlands Filmmuseum and the National Film Center of Tokyo, but by now the bottom of the barrel is all but naked to view. Film festivals are increasingly aggressive ('what unknown treasure can we spring this time?'), because archives have been spoiling them for years. When the gold has been mined to a fare-thee-well, the Forty-niner packs up and goes home to count what was all along locked in the safe.

4) Restoring a badly damaged film takes a lot of time and money. Film restoration worth the name requires vast amounts of patience and dedication. However great the benefits may be to future generations, it may lack instant gratification for the intelligentsia of the present. Few benefactors will give film preservation their unconditional support. They want to know what is to be restored, and to be assured that, once restored, they will like it, or at least that it will appeal to large audiences. Non-fiction shorts of the early years? No thanks, but how about some Greta Garbo? Incidentally, one thing our successors are sure to inherit is the ability to show no more than a tiny fraction of what has been preserved. More than 95% of what is now in the

archives will continue their (not so peaceful) slumbers on our shelves. Whether we like it or not, the greatest conservative in this game is the public. And the public is always right when government officials regard it as a potential electorate. What answer can there be to that subtle form of blackmail, given the cost of the endeavour: several thousand dollars per reel of film. For the sake of some highly visible (even though in the long run irrelevant) project, donors may be willing to throw money out the window for the sheer conspicuousness of the gesture, but they draw the line at preserving obscure titles, worthy though they may be. The commercial laboratories to which naïve or opportunistic professionals bring their copies sometimes work in haste, on the premise that few will know the difference between a really good print and a mediocre dupe. A single negative is a less than ideal option for colour preservation. A separation negative (consisting as it does of three masters, one for each primary colour) is far more stable, but it costs three times as much as a standard print and occupies three times the space in the vault. In an enterprise so costly in every way, no wonder so few colour films have been restored with the most adequate technology. Nor is it any wonder that the existing preservation copies are fading away like any standard colour print, only more slowly. Curators are well aware of this, but dislike mentioning it for fear of jeopardising their funding.

5) As often happens when a valid principle is applied too literally, the notion that each print is an original with its own historical identity can be an excuse for an unjustifiable expenditure of time, money and energy. If a certain American film survives in a single copy found in the Netherlands, and has Dutch intertitles, it is needless to say a good plan to restore it as is, lest we otherwise be unable to see it at all. But if that same film is already fully preserved in its American release version, and still another copy of it survives with titles in a different language but much shorter in length, I fail to see the rationale of restoring it once again. It is sometimes argued that such a restoration is justified because the film was originally seen by another audience in a different form. But after all, how far are we willing to carry that principle? Applying it in an indiscriminate way can be wasteful and ridiculous. In the late 01990s there was an uproar over the duplication by the Cinémathèque française of a heavily abridged nitrate print of *Chicago*, a film produced by Cecil B. DeMille and co-directed by Fred Urson and Paul Iribe

in 01928. A beautiful and very complete print with original intertitles can be found at the UCLA Film and Television Archive in Los Angeles. In reply to protests at the redundancy of the project the archive explained that the short version of this American film was an artifact of French culture because of its original distribution in France in that form. And the reply is correct in the literal sense that the term 'national film heritage' should not be limited to the films actually produced within its distribution territory. In just that way, the Jean Desmet collection, a remarkable corpus of 920 titles made between 01906 and 01936 consisting mainly of non-Dutch productions, is unquestionably part of the Dutch film heritage because of the role played by these films in the history of film distribution in the Netherlands plus its status as a coherent, self-contained constellation of prints. Well and good. But consider the 50-minute American version of *Cabiria* held by the Museum of Modern Art in New York. MoMA does well to protect this drastic abridgement of Pastrone's historical epic, yet imagine what the response would be if it were to announce a new restoration of it. Most people would prefer to see the version restored by the Museo Nazionale del Cinema in Turin at 183 minutes and 16 frames per second, and who could quarrel with them. Yet is so happens that the MoMA print contains a crucial shot (of a naked child held by a pair of hands toward some raging flames) missing from the standard version of Turin until the mid-01990s. Indeed it was the discovery of that shot that persuaded the Turin archive that a new restoration of *Cabiria* was in order.

All very sensible and rational. In the meantime, while some festival advertises the premiere of a new version of *The Absolute Masterpiece*®, thousands of nitrate reels agonise on their shelves. We are left to wonder whether this cycle of thinking can ever be broken. As regards that situation, the author of this collection of aphorisms is as shrewd in his diagnosis as he is vague about the corrective steps to be taken. I see only one course of action that can be effective: the creation of a registry of unpreserved films, compiled by a consortium of public and private institutions, small and large, taking upon itself the responsibility of seeing that the list is circulated and read by the largest number of people, and in the kindest way in the world, yet firmly, refusing to entertain a single restoration project, however well supported by newspaper headlines, which might indirectly condemn other less well known films to slow death in the vaults. A consortium that would encourage the review of the policies and procedures that govern the task of preservation in the archives, and that would recommend standards as precise as the ones observed in similar institutions dealing with the fine arts. A consortium that would urge its members to deny restoration projects to laboratories that fail to meet the exacting parameters required (and whose incompetence, by the way, can perpetuate the spiraling phenomenon of the archival remake). A consortium that at long last would help to end the deadly and wasteful confusion that exists between administrative duties, fundraising, and curatorial responsibility. One that would prevent the archives from falling into the hands of those trained in the latest fashions of management science but illiterate in film, or vice versa. And most important, a consortium that would not be dictated to about what should or should not be done with the images that have survived, one, in short, that would insist that film curators and development officers continue to exist as integrated but separate professional entities whose operations are geared to the enrichment of posterity and not exclusively to the ephemeral glory of some splashy event, however apt to attract funding.

Digital culture has become the latest arena in which continues the old debate on what curatorial expertise should render to Caesar and what to God. But surely an effort at specifying what its proper uses and limitations may be would put both sides of the argument into sharper focus. Much as we have learned to fight against those who would have us jettison altogether those frail but cumbersome artifacts called film prints, we should be no less adamant with those who reject all kinds of technological advance in the name of tradition and out of a misplaced sense of historical integrity. The issue cannot be defined either in terms of a blind utopian faith in what the future will bring or in those of a purism so narrow that it rejects outright the intervention of electronics into areas where it has never existed. The real issues transcend either of those romantic attitudes. Two considerations ought to be kept in mind. The first is that perversion of the democratic ideal into which the larger issues of the guardianship of a cultural heritage has inserted a mistaken notion of the right to public access. Many of those who are unaware of the operations of a moving image archive are under the impression that a film available on video is actually preserved somewhere.

They are the first to transfer their parents' home movies onto tape and then discard the originals. We've all heard them: 'Hey, I can watch them on my computer. Why don't you do likewise? What's the big deal? Why spend a fortune on conservation? Didn't you just say they'll decompose just the same? They're not yours anyway. They belong to the Hollywood majors, so let them do it.' There is an element of truth in this: the archives can see the advantage of sparing their precious prints the wear and tear of projection by making them available in other forms, and it carries the additional attractions of egalitarianism (easy access for all) and cost-effectiveness (cheaper reference copies). But by yielding to it we lend ourselves to the situation of the tourists who spend a day in line waiting to see Cézanne, follow it by a twenty-minute stroll through the galleries, and cap it off by going to the gift shop to pick up a poster of their favorite painting. It is a ritual that pays lip service to the duty of educating the public, even while encouraging to its Been There, Done That. And who can blame them?

The second point to be stressed is that a viable answer is yet to be found to the obsolescence created by every new hardware system. The best solution we've been able to arrive at so far is to duplicate all moving images from one system to another before the new technology has thoroughly killed its predecessor. The very discussion of whether or not digital technology (for example) will allow us to transfer all the decaying film into digital form, preserve it as such for an indefinite period of time, and then convert it back to film again is self-delusory. For even if it were technically feasible – and, for the present at least, it is not economically so – there are technologies of the moving image that will not lend themselves to such a proceeding. How to preserve artworks made on cd-rom? What techniques should be used to restore video games? Will there eventually be a museum to preserve the moving and speaking images available through the world wide web? (To the best of my knowledge, the Library of Congress is still alone among public institutions in experimenting with that idea by saving all the world's websites once a month. The drawback that makes this preservation project inaccessible to the user is that there is a good deal of pornography in it.) It is not surprising that a good 80% of the films produced during the silent period are lost. The percentage of loss of motion pictures made within the last ten years will exceed even that. The future holds escalating percentages of loss, for production is rising at such a rate that the best efforts at preservation will soon be a drop in the bucket. We will be unable even to estimate the number of moving images lost because there will be no way of knowing how many there had been.

Amid all this confusion, lab technicians can only respond with a nervous giggle to the latest cause to be unearthed for the imminent decay and loss of motion picture stock, one of the many deaths of cinema we have been hearing about since 01920. They are all aware that the entertainment industry won't risk its money on films it will be unable to exploit because of another hi-tech turnover. Their promises of new webs, lasers and satellites are made to a consumer who will shell out hard cash to acquire them once the market research indicates the time is ripe. Film stock will continue to be produced for a while, if only for master elements such as camera negatives. The reasons for the survival of this nineteenth-century invention are easy enough to find. The uses and potential of 35mm are well-nigh infinite. You can transfer it to whatever you please, and you needn't concern yourself with technological change for the simple reason that photographic film is such a simple object, so simple that is hasn't descended into obsolescence in over a hundred years and, better yet, you don't need much equipment to see its images. Computer programmes become hieroglyphs within a short time, but you'll always be able to build a projector and make a screen. All you need is a light source, a lens and a shutter plus a large white surface.

But if you really want to know what the final chapter will be of your aphoristic author's unfinished manuscript, let me tell you. The day will come (and sooner than you think) when 35mm film will no longer be made because Hollywood will no longer need it, and there will be absolutely nothing that anyone can do about it. What company would willingly maintain a complex and costly facility for a handful of institutions whose demand for archival film stock would not even meet the cost of its operations? Unable to preserve cinema by means of cinema, the archives (no doubt after a few pathetic gestures such as proposing to manufacture film for their own use) will be forced to face up to reality and go for other options. Projecting a film will become first a special circumstance, then a rare occurrence, and finally an exceptional event. Eventually nothing at all will be projected, either because all surviving copies will be worn to a frazzle or decomposed, or because somebody decides to stop showing them in order to save for future duplication onto another format the few prints that remain. There will be a final screening attended by a final audience, perhaps indeed a lonely spectator. With that, cinema will be talked about and written about as some remote hallucination, a dream that lasted a century or two. Future generations will be hard put to understand why so many people spent their lives in an effort to resuscitate that dream.

If all this comes to pass, our successors will have to face once again, though under different conditions, the same dilemmas that face us. Shall they try to preserve all moving images or only some of them? The answer may lie in another question. Must a museum cover the entire history of art, from prehistoric scratches on bones to Damien Hirst, to justify its existence? Museums exist of the arts of ancient Greece, of pre-Columbian pottery, of French Impressionists, of Medieval sculpture. Which most of us accept. Then why not accept the idea of one archive devoted exclusively to cinema, another to video, and on and on? Still, the notion of a Louvre of the moving image holds a powerful attraction for us, possibly because we pretend that moving images are too young for a specialised history. Which is a great pity. Before long, circumstances may force us to modify our ambitions and see how well we can operate the equivalent of a Musée du Jeu de Paume. A century of cinema is more than enough to cope with. There would be plenty of work for everyone for years to come.

In the short run (in accordance with the tendency to see film and video as separate forms of expression despite their mutual influences) the distinctions among the various components of a museum might even resolve themselves within the same archival institution. It might please us to think of it as a producer, a research centre, a permanent encyclopedia, a publisher, a school for professional training despite the risk implicit in a proliferation of goals, in doing a bit of everything while nothing gets done. But it should be acknowledged that the discipline of moving image preservation has resolved itself into at least two practical philosophies: the institution that features a single specialty, be it conservation (Library of Congress), programming (Cinémathèque française), archival training (George Eastman House) or devotion to a single theme (Imperial War Museum), and the one that aims at a synthesis of a variety of functions

(British Film Institute). But they have a common tendency towards a concept of cinema as a special event. Instead of steadily declining as repertory houses of permanent education, they might yet become institutions of the special attraction. The cult of the director's cut has already given us *Touch of Evil* as Orson Welles intended it, and *The Wild Bunch* with the alternate ending; the ideology of the longer version has already given us *Nights of Cabiria* and *Rocco and His Brothers* before the cuts; interest in bringing classic cinema to new audiences has already given us *Vertigo* in its Dolby Digital version. The filmgoing experience has already assumed something of the mystique surrounding an opera event. A younger generation will come to the theatre because of its curiosity about the strengths of the big screen, or because it has discovered that the promise of a Global Cinematheque in electronic form is a delusion, for what would the demand be for the complete works of Allan Dwan on their home computer? The notion that a digital or satellite library would make it possible to browse through an entire history of cinema on our monitors is an astonishing misconception, failing as it does to recognise the realities of a mass of obscure motion pictures that only a handful of people will ever want to see and even fewer distributors will bother making accessible for cash. And even if they did, too many films would be kept out of public consumption because of their uncertain legal status.

Copyright control was born from the intention of protecting and promoting rights of individual creativity. That noble concern has now degenerated into an obscene legal construct for the furtherance of economic power. The producers of a film are usually its owners, although in some countries the moral claims of its other contributors – such as directors, writers, performers, cinematographers, composers – are also asserted and protected, a prerogative that sometimes becomes hereditary, descending to families and heirs. Once upon a time films were abandoned or destroyed after their commercial release. Now they are cultural treasures. But who was it after all who rescued them from oblivion and loss? An archive may own a copy of a film without enjoying the right to exhibit it. As if the intervention that prevented its disappearance were a theft to be forgiven!

A good question for the owners and proprietors of moral rights would be: where were you when Henri Langlois and Jacques Ledoux and James Card were paying out of their own slim resources to avoid seeing tons of nitrate film loaded into dumpsters? Would not mere justice have required that they be reimbursed? Have you no responsibility for the costs incurred in fifty years of preservation and storage? Is that not a moral right of no less weight than your own? It was their choice to preserve films without seeking permission. Nobody forced them to do it, and there is some legitimacy in their right to go on doing it without being treated like burglars. No one will deny the legitimacy of copyright for the encouragement of cultural industry in the 19th century, but today its uneven application is an obstruction to that very purpose, and the unavailing struggle against the illegal duplication of moving images through the electronic media shows how urgent is the need for some other framework, some legal control of creativity that doesn't inhibit creativity itself. The time must come when the rights to moving images made for commercial purposes must give way to the claims of history. It is not a new idea that a pluralist society must be able to promote culture as a driving force of its economy, and not the other way around.

And so it happens that moving image archives are keenest to preserve the films that have fallen into the public domain. They existed long before the paranoia of copyright prevailed over common sense. Other films of recent make go under the name of 'orphans' in the archives, either because their production companies no longer exist or because of an oversight of copyright renewal. Either the relatives of directors and performers are dead, or it never occurred to them to assert their claims. Should these films be allowed to crumble to dust because they are of no monetary value? How are the archives to understand their own reason for existing? Are they responsible for what should have been done by others, or wait till the last possible minute to follow the dictates of conscience? If that's all copyright is good for, then let it be damned. What use and justice does it have? Future generations may have to wait before seeing the films, but their legal owners should be forced to wait with them. Let them bring us to court. We are eager for an opportunity to publicise this monstrous inequity. Let them prohibit public access. Patience is the archivist's first virtue, and the copyright predators will learn what patience is when they are confronted with the task of exploiting moving images as lots of real estate. We can wait, but meanwhile shall we or shall we not preserve them?

THE DEATH OF CINEMA

Which is exactly what our predecessors did at a time when nobody would listen to them. It may even be good for us to do it again for a while, provided we remember that all our talk about budgets and legal rights, about the digital age and the vinegar syndrome is meaningless if it does not preserve a thing that is no less precious than moving images themselves, the right to see them. Seeing is an art unto itself. And absolutely nothing compels us to turn what is for us a passion into a business. We may succumb to that temptation now and then, when our goals require it. But let us put an end to all this angst over the end of cinema. I have no particular fondness for Bruce Chatwin's writings, but I do find there are some accurate hits about museums in his fictional work, and his idea of dismantling them every fifty years in order to restore life to the objects they contain has some interest and appeal. Life is short, and cinema won't last forever. But for now it's still here. It may become something else, but so what if it does? There are worse things. Physical pain. Not enough food, or none at all. Being alone. Losing interest in the art of seeing. If we want cinema to exist a few more years, let us first preserve the good things that make it one of life's enrichments. There is a chance of succeeding as long as we can accept the paradox that a film screening in a museum, contrary to what it has been as a popular art and entertainment for over a century, is a gala soirée with a boosted price of admission and a certain amount of formality. I don't wear neckties to them, except to the ones you attend.

REPLY

Sir,

Yes, I will certainly publish the manuscript you have returned to me, despite what you call its arrogance and my own doubts about the benefits it may render (for nobody in the world ever truly sees anything he hasn't personally paid for) and despite those readers who will be encouraged to think that they have at last encountered the Model Image or at any rate have come close to seeing it themselves. But I find it worth publishing it for the sake of its testimony to the fragility of human vision.

If it has any instructive lesson, there is one for viewers themselves, for it shows that all lost moving images have at least existed for some viewer in the past. The unseen is an integral part of our lives, even if not directly our own. I well remember the experience of hearing Kevin Brownlow describe the lovely tinted and toned nitrate print of *The Blue Bird* (Maurice Tourneur, 01918) he had seen years earlier. Listening to him I could understand something of its loss: it might have existed as recently as twenty years ago, and I might have seen it. Still, I can feel no despair over it. No exhaustive filmography of lost cinema will ever be possible, and I'm quite satisfied to leave it at that. The fact that the unseen is beyond our control is an excellent antidote to our claim to authority over the visible world, and administers a good shaking up to our deluded obsession with permanence. Sooner or later you and I will both disappear, along with our visions and memories of what we have seen and the way we have seen it. Don't deceive yourself.

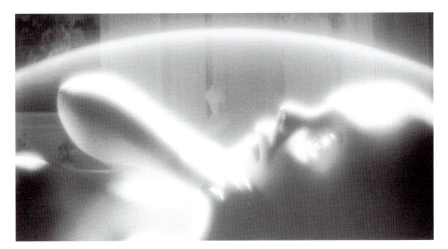

The final sequence of *2001: A Space Odyssey* (Stanley Kubrick, 01968) stirred countless speculations on its 'message'. Early reviews complained about the non-narrative structure of the film, lamenting the fact that audiences could not understand the director's intentions. In rejecting this approach, Kubrick told an interviewer that 'once you're dealing on a non-verbal level, ambiguity is unavoidable. But it's the ambiguity of all art, a fine piece of music or a painting – you don't need written instructions by the composer or painter accompanying such works to "explain" them. "Explaining" them contributes nothing but a superficial "cultural" value which has no value except for critics and teachers who have to earn a living ... In this sense, the film becomes anything the viewer sees in it.' (Joseph Gelmis, *The Film Director as Superstar* [New York: Doubleday, 01970], pp. 303–304.)

The concept of a film history based on a regressio ad infinitum *– that is, from an image that has completely vanished to its theoretical inception as a Model Image – is germane to an understanding of film history itself as a cultural artifact. However, a reverse narrative leading from a factual nonentity (an image that has been lost forever) to its potential counterpart (an image existing before being seen for the first time) makes it difficult to use the term 'history' at all. The inquiry into the past of the moving image should then be redefined not so much as an attempt to explain the causes of its transformation but as an endless journey into the unachieved potential of the image itself and the intentions of its maker.*

NOTE

A stone carving in the Qobustan plateau of Azerbaijan shows a dog attacking a wild boar, one of the earliest known representations of movement. As an artifact it may not be as old as the Venus of Willendorf or the Çatal Hüyük mural paintings, but its sheer survival for several thousand years in an extreme climate of harsh winds and endless storms from the Caspian Sea, despite no effort to preserve it, summarises better than anything I can think of the questions addressed in the texts printed here. In the fall of 01986, at a time that was witnessing an international resurgence in the culture and practices of film preservation, the author submitted some methodological notes under the heading *Une Image modèle* to the editors of the French journal of film theory *Hors Cadre*, which were eventually published in its 6th issue (01988) in a typographical form slightly different from the original Italian text. Since then, the essay has grown through a series of revisions and rewrites documented by printings in the Dutch journal *Versus* [Nijmegen] Issue 1, 01988 and in *Cinegrafie* [Bologna], Vol. I, No. 1, 01989, as well as in other publications, sometimes under different titles. The sixth draft presented here is only a further crystallisation of the same process, inasmuch as its concept, structure and development are to some extent a direct reflection of the issues addressed in it. Other versions – complete, excerpted or translated, always with some variations – are to be found in an early sketch of the *Hors Cadre* essay, published in *Segnocinema* [Vicenza], Vol. III, No. 8, May 01983; *Sight and Sound*, Vol. 56, No. 3, summer 01987; *Segnocinema*, Vol. XVI, No. 82, November-December 01996; Rick Fell (ed.), *Footage: The Worldwide Moving Image Sourcebook* (New York: Second Line Search, 01997); Matti Lukkarila, Olavi Similä and Sakari Toiviainen (eds.), *Filmin Tähden. Suomen elokuva-arkisto 40 vuotta* (Helsinki: Suomen elokuva-arkisto, 01997); *The Stanford Humanities Review*, Vol. 7, No. 2, Winter 01999; *L'ultimo spettatore* (Milan: Editrice Il Castoro, 01999).

ABOUT THE AUTHOR

Paolo Cherchi Usai, senior curator of the Motion Picture Department at George Eastman House, is associate professor of Film at the University of Rochester and director of the L. Jeffrey Selznick School of Film Preservation, established in 1996. Co-founder of the Pordenone Silent Film Festival and Domitor (Society for Early Cinema Studies), he is an adjunct member of the National Film Preservation Board, and a member of the Executive Committee of the International Federation of Film Archives (FIAF). His latest book is *Silent Cinema: An Introduction* (BFI Publishing, 2000).